The Time Is Now!

Activating Kingdom Wealth In Your Life!

EBONY MOORE

ISBN-13: 978-1-963424-41-6

DEDICATION

May these words encourage and motivate you to excel
beyond your greatest potential.

CONTENTS

ACKNOWLEDGMENTS

Without God, nothing is possible

INTRODUCTION

Do you feel weighed down by your circumstances? Do you feel stuck?

Are you frustrated with your financial status? Do you feel like your hands are tied and life has just given you a bad apple?

Do you often get mad at yourself because you know you can change your financial situation, but haven't? Do you often wonder what is holding you back from taking steps forward to accomplish your dreams?

If you answered yes to any of the above questions it is time to change your current situation and propel into your divine destiny!

God never created you to be in poverty! His will for you is to be healthy and prosper, even as your soul prospers. He created you with a special purpose in mind!

Whether you know it or not, God created you in His image and equipped you with everything you need to be successful in life. God deposited unique gifts and talents that compose the purpose for which He created you.

That dead-end job is not the end for you! Multiple streams of income can become a reality! All you have to do is take a step of faith! Believe you can do all things through Christ who strengthens you! Get up from depression, low self-esteem, past failures, and mistakes. Move forward into your destiny now!

2 Kings 7:1-8 gives a formula for success. These scriptures let us know that we each possess the ability to make a decision that can change the course of our lives.

2 Kings 7:1 Then Elisha said, Hear ye the word of the Lord; Thus saith the LORD, Tomorrow about this time shall a measure of fine flour be sold for a shekel, and two measures of fine flour be sold for a shekel, and two measures of barley for a shekel, in the gate of Samaria. 2 Ki 7:2 Then a lord on whose hand the king leaned answered the man of God, and said, Behold, if the LORD would make windows in heaven, might this thing be? And he said, Behold, thou shalt see it with thine eyes, but shall not eat thereof. 2 Ki 7:3 And there were four leprous men at the entering of the gate; and they said one to another, Why sit here until we die there: and if we sit still here, we die also. Now therefore come, and let us fall unto the host of the Syrians: if they save us alive, we shall live; and if they kill us, we shall but die. 2Ki 7:5 And they rose up in the twilight, to go unto the camp of the Syrians: and when they were come to the uttermost part of the camp of Syria, behold there was no man there. 2 Ki 7:6 For the Lord had made the host of the Syrians hear a noise of horses, even the noise of a great host: and they said one to another, Lo, the king of Israel hath hired against us the kings of Hittites, and the kings of the Egyptians to come to us. 2 Ki 7:7 Wherefore they arose and fled in the twilight, and left their asses, even the camp as it was, and fled for their life. 2Ki 7:8 And these lepers came to the uttermost part of the camp, they went into one tent and did eat and drink, and carried thence silver, and gold, and raiment, and went and hid it. (*2 Kings 7:1-8 KJV*)

This passage of scripture shows the key points: (1) There was a severe famine in the land (2) This famine affected everything – communication, the economic climate, and food (3) The tenacity of the lepers. In the passage, the four lepers sat outside of the gate of Syria contemplating a life-and death-decision. Going into the city would mean they would be risking their lives because they were lepers and they were not allowed to enter civilization. On the other hand, they knew if they continued to do nothing they would die. Change came for the leper men when they decided to take a chance and try to change their situation even if death was presented! These four men made a decision to move forward and press past fears. They took s risk and decided to see what was on the other side of the gate to the city. Can you imagine what kind of faith and courage it took for these men to enter Syria? As soon as they made up their mind to act they discovered that provision had already been made.

The Lord has also made these same provisions for you. God is waiting for someone to believe Him and take Him at His Word! If you take one step of faith, God will meet you halfway!

The leprous men made a decision to move and not remain in a *deadly* situation. Let's just be honest and say they made a decision to do "something" rather than do "nothing" at all.

What desperate situation are you in right now? When will you stop making excuses for not pursuing your dreams? When will you trust God?

Right now we are in a time when God desires to pour down blessings like never before. You must believe you have greatness inside you! God has equipped you with gifts, and talents that have the potential to bring you great prosperity. Believe the visions and promises God has shown you, then act upon them.

What idea has God given you? Maybe He's given you an idea for an invention! You may have books, plays, or a new sound of music locked in you waiting for an opportunity to get out. Has he given you a new department to start in your local ministry? Whatever He has given you, it's time to move to action! Your dreams can come true! It's time to take your dreams off the shelf and get to work! Why sit here until you die?

Try God at His Word! Make the decision to get up and get started! It's time for you to prosper! The time is now!!!!

CHAPTER ONE

DO YOU KNOW YOUR PURPOSE?

The purpose of life is a life of purpose.
-Robert Byrne

Knowing your purpose is an important factor in obtaining a happy, fulfilling, and successful life. Many people live unfulfilling and depressing lives because they do not pursue their purpose. As a result, they become locked in a world of regret and failure.

This doesn't have to be you! You can change your situation! You can change your destiny! The power to change it lies within you!

The first thing you must do is figure out your purpose. Everything on earth has a purpose for existence. When we find out what our purpose is our lives become more meaningful. Discovering your purpose will help you identify your goals and motivate you to action. Your purpose will inspire you to unlock and maximize your potential.

If you don't know what your purpose is, you can start by asking yourself "What am I passionate about?" Your passion is something you have a strong desire, liking, or interest in or a particular gift, skill, or talent.

Here are a few good points that will help you identify your passion:

1) **Your passion is something you enjoy doing!** You have a desire to do it even if it means you won't get paid for it. It can also be a skill that you develop.

Matter-of-fact, you spend endless hours doing it because doing it is a stress releaser for you.

2) **Your passion is something that appears effortless to you!** Others have to work hard to perform this function but it comes naturally to you! Your friends or co-workers probably tell you how good you are at using this gift. They may even tell you have successful you would be if you operated in this gifting full-time.

3) **You can do this skill for long periods of time.** You lose track of time while using this gift. Sometimes you find yourself putting other obligations on the shelf just so you can do this thing you are so passionate about!

4) **You feel happy when you are using this gift!** You love doing this thing. Everything about you changes when you are using this gift! When you are doing what you are passionate about you have a great attitude. You want to tell everything you have learned and/or experienced while using this gift! It's something you never get tired of talking about.

Passion is where your success lies. Your passion is what will drive you to success.

Passion will push you!

Passion will make you stay up an hour extra each night so you can accomplish your goal.

Passion will create vision.

IT'S IN YOU!

When I was five years old I remember walking around the house telling my parents that I was going to be an author. I spent my free time drawing and creating short stories. By the time I was in middle school, I was writing short novels and plays. I stayed up many nights writing and creating fictional characters and scenes.

I loved to make up stories. It was as if I was watching the pages come alive before my eyes. I was fascinated with this unique ability I possessed to create stories from my imagination.

I wrote for many years before I finally realized that writing was actually my purpose. I worked job after job even though I knew I had no future there. At 27 years old I suffered sensorineural hearing loss and suddenly became deaf in my right ear. It took months to learn to function with one ear. I had to stay in bed until the auditory nerve in my brain healed. I decided to make the most of my time and began writing and illustrating children's books on my laptop. Creating these books temporarily took my mind off my hearing loss, disappointments, and worries. To my surprise, my skills increased and before I knew it, I had already written and illustrated ten children's books. I began to think how wonderful it would be if I could write and illustrate for a living.

Hearing loss caused me to gain knowledge of my purpose. Writing and illustrating was an ability that was locked away inside of me. I now have nearly forty titles in print, my own cartoon character, and MYA KIDS, LLC, a company that distributes children's books globally. Writing and illustrating is in me. What is the gift that is in you? God used something that appeared to be devastating to uncover my purpose. Romans 8:28 says that **all things work together** *for good to them that love God, to them who are the called according to his purpose.* What obstacles have you faced? God can turn tragedy into triumph and turn it around for His glory. Maybe that trial or obstacle you faced was meant to propel you into purpose. I challenge you to discover the gifts that are locked away in you at all costs!

STAY IN YOUR LANE!

I heard a pastor preach a series of life-changing sermons on "using your gifts." Throughout these sermons, he emphasized "Stay in your lane! Your gifting is your lane!" It appeared as if he was climbing over chairs to get this message across to his congregation. He told us that once we understood what our gifts were, to stick with it, perfect it, and we would find great success in that area.

At the time, I remember thinking I was "staying in my lane" and doing a pretty good job at it. I knew I was created to create children's books and even though I wasn't being as diligent in distributing them to schools as I could have, I was still doing *something.*
Weeks later, I was a little depressed about the lack of attention my children's books were receiving. Years earlier, God instructed me not to go to a traditional publisher, but to self-publish my own titles and start a company with my own cartoon character from the ground level.

By then I had written and illustrated over 30 titles, but they were not getting the attention I expected. I had some successful ventures and some that were unsuccessful.

Sometimes schools would welcome me and absolutely love the character education children's series I'd created. Others seemed to talk of all the ways they would help me get them into different agencies, libraries, and schools. But I never heard from them again.

I knew the purpose of the children's books was to build self-esteem, character education, and development in children. God had given me an awesome purpose, gift, passion, and a vision to change the world through these books. I understood the importance of global distribution but I was becoming frustrated with those who didn't.

It's amazing what a person will do out of frustration. In my frustration, I did the very thing God told me not to do. I contacted an associate at a big-name traditional publisher and asked her if she would visit my website and look at my books. A week went by before I received a reply from her in an email. It read:

"Dear Ebony,"
"I Hope you are well! Thank you for considering our company for your publishing needs. While your illustrations are unique, your style is different than what we are accustomed to. We wish you all the success in this great endeavor and sincerely hope you find a home for your vision."

This email discouraged me a little. Shortly after reading it a good friend and colleague from Florida called to give me pointers on how to launch marketing strategies for my children's books and cartoon character "Mya." He asked me how things were going with the children's books and I told him all about my experience with the big-name publishing company. I shared with him how I'd gotten frustrated and decided to try to sign with a traditional publisher only to be rejected.

He cut my words off and reiterated the pastor's words, "Stay in your lane!" I was shocked, and then he said "You are trying to be successful at what somebody else did and that isn't going to work for you! Don't you know that big-name publishers are dinosaurs in this industry? At one time they were a valuable commodity but they are not now. They were and are very good at what they do but it was only for a set time. Now it's your time! Stay in your lane! They are not going to see the vision God gave you because it is not for them to see. They are blinded by what you have created. God doesn't want them to see it, but rather for you to get up and get it out there! Do you understand what I am saying?" His statement caused me to realize that I was not staying in my lane at all.

My colleague continued to aggressively talk to me and I knew God was using him to get the message over to me. He hadn't come to my church and heard the sermons had preached on staying in your lane. As a matter-of-fact, he was halfway across the United States of America!

"Now listen, they are occupying space that belongs to you! What God has given you is new oil. Remember it's your time! You have to get out there and make it happen! It's not going to just come to you! Put the work in! We are self-made millionaires in this season and hour! If you want it, it's yours for the taking! Stay in your lane!" He said again.

I hung up the phone. I was excited, motivated, and back on track. From that moment on, I knew the only way I was going to be successful was if I stayed in my own lane, the lane that God designed me to function. I would have to learn to work through my frustrations and be more believing and obedient in doing what God had so instructed me to do.

Once you find out what your purpose is, stay in your lane. Moving out of your lane is like trying to fit a puzzle piece into the wrong place. Have you ever purchased the wrong-sized battery to fit in your remote control? The remote was only designed to work with a certain size or kind of battery!

You and I were designed for a specific purpose! We work best when we operate in that area. Make up your mind that you are going to stay in your lane. It will eliminate frustration and aimlessness. We become frustrated when we don't stay in our lane. We become even more frustrated when we try to operate in someone else's lane.

Remember, your passion is where your heart is. When you find where your passion lies, you'll find what treasures God has set up for you! Find your purpose and stay in your lane so you can fulfill your destiny!

CHAPTER TWO

YOU ARE THE MOUNTAIN

**"The biggest mountains we must move are
the ones in our own minds." ~E. MOORE**

UNTIE YOURSELF, YOU GREAT BIG
ELEPHANT!!!

Have you ever heard the story "The Elephant in the
Circus?" It's about an elephant that had been tied to a pole
with a rope when it was very young by its trainer. Naturally,
the elephant doesn't like being tied to anything and tries to
escape several times, but the rope and the pole are too strong.
After a while, the elephant eventually gives up trying to
escape.

Later on, when it is older, the elephant still believes it
cannot escape from the rope and remains in the same place,
despite the fact it could easily escape.

In this story, instead of the big elephant breaking free, he
stands there obedient to the bondage of the rope. The rope
not only had the elephant's leg trapped, but also his mind.
The elephant's mind was the mountain. The hurdle
of failure was imprinted in his mind and blinded him from
seeing his own great potential.

This is what many people do today. Many people are tied
to the same pole of failure, fear, disappointment, and doubt
with a tiny little rope. This rope keeps them in bondage. The
rope is a representation of how you see yourself, your

self-esteem, and your lack of belief that God has uniquely made you to carry out His Will. You must remember that you already have the victory! Jesus overcame the world and the devil does not have the power to stop you! Luke 10:19 confirms our victorious defeat over the devil.

> Behold, I give unto you power to tread on
> serpents and scorpions, and over all the power
> of the enemy: and nothing shall by any means
> hurt you. -Luke 10:19

This scripture means the devil is not able to stop you. God lives inside of you and with God on your side you cannot be defeated! Quite frankly, the only way you can be stopped is when you stop yourself! More often than not, you are your own worst enemy!

I have often studied this scripture found in Mark 11:23-24.

> "For verily I say unto you, That whosoever
> shall say unto this mountain, Be thou removed,
> and be thou cast into the sea; and shall not
> doubt in his heart, but shall believe that those
> things which he saith shall come to pass; he
> shall have whatsoever he saith. Therefore I say
> unto you, what things soever ye desire when ye
> pray, believe that ye receive them, and ye shall
> have them.

The more I began to ask God to give me the understanding about what this scripture means. He began to show me that sometimes the mountains are not big old invisible demons, but negative lies the enemy has told us about ourselves. They say things like:

You can't do it. You don't have the experience. You're not

smart enough. You don't deserve it. You are not good enough, etc.

In most cases, the "you" in all of these statements has been replaced with the letter "I". So you begin to hear "I can't do it. I don't have the experience. I'm not smart enough, I don't deserve it! I'm not good enough, etc.

Since we were all born in a world of sin, we have heard these thoughts all of our lives and after a while we generally believe what we have heard repeatedly. And instead of combating these lies we add to the devils strategic plan to ruin us. We ignorantly say what we hear, causing our words and thoughts to become an inescapable reality. However, these statements or thoughts do not line up with the Word of God. We cannot believe the report of the enemy. These are the mountains that we must speak to in order to untie ourselves from our small rope.

The great news is, unlike the elephant, we can untie ourselves from the limitations of our minds! We do this by believing the promises found in God's Word. In His Word, he tells us that all things are possible through Christ who strengthens us! He also tells us that faith cometh by hearing and hearing the Word of God, Romans 10:17. These are just a few of the many promises found in God's Word.

At times, we all find ourselves struggling to believe what God said about us. That's why we have to allow God to change the way we have been programmed to think. Our minds have been trained to believe negative over positive.

Here is a helpful scripture from the Bible that clearly confirms that our minds must be renewed or made like new.

Do not be conformed to this world, but be transformed by the renewal of your mind, that by testing you may discern what is the will of God, what is good and acceptable and perfect."
Romans 12:2

God says you are above and never beneath! He says that you are the head and not the tail!

TAKING RESPONSIBILITY FOR WHAT'S IN YOUR MIND

By now hopefully you understand that you have to take responsibility for what's in your mind. If you tell the truth you've had some thoughts that have kept you from being successful. Maybe those thoughts have been robbing you of fulfilling your purpose and the wealth God designed for you.

What's in your mind is very important because it determines your every action. Your mind tells your body what to do.

EDUCATION

If you want be successful, begin to educate yourself in the Word of God. Read and get to know who God is. Reading the Bible will help you grow and develop your relationship with God. It will help you hear and recognize when He is giving you encouragement and instructions to carry out His will for your life.

Educating yourself in God's Word will begin the renewal process in your mind.

YOU ARE WHO YOU HANG AROUND

Remember, you are who you hang around. Take a good look at all those around you daily. If they are not headed in a positive direction or the direction you want to go, you are going to have to change your acquaintances.

You do not need people around you that are negatively impacting your future. You have to feed yourself with positive people and thoughts. If you want to be successful in life you need to get around people who are already successful or working towards doing something positive in their life. Avoid people without vision, lack of focus, self-worth and self-control. Their aimlessness will only bring you down.

DIVINE MENTORSHIP

There are great benefits to having a mentor. My mentors helped me walk through many different obstacles and see areas in my life that needed improvement. You need someone who knows when to encourage you and when to correct you.

A mentor is different than a good friend because a friend will tolerate you and love you the way you are, but a mentor will push you to move beyond your comfort zone.

A mentor will challenge you in every area of your life. Mentors can see your strengths and weaknesses. A mentor's job is to help you maximize your potential. A mentor will pull on the gifts you possess.

The mentor can only succeed in their job if you are willing to relinquish control and receive their advice. You must submit yourself to the direction of the mentor and not become offended when they are pointing out flawed areas. If you don't have a mentor, ask God to send one into your life.

Note: When the mentor comes, make sure to spend time praying for him/her. That person is going to have to help you through your stubbornness and blind spots. You know more than anyone that you are a real piece of work!

Previously I shared how God used mentors to help me get my life on track. I became frustrated when people did not respond to my books immediately. As a result I got angry and chose to deal with the situation out of frustration. Soon after, I realized that frustration with other people was unjust. God had given me vision and instruction on the books, not the people I became frustrated with. It was my job to push the children's books globally, not someone else's! Sure God would send people with resources to help me and even people with the capacity to bless me financially in this endeavor. But the books weren't moving because I wasn't moving. In this situation I was the mountain.

I was the only one who could stop what God had designed for me and the only way it wouldn't come to pass was if I didn't move into action.

You may have tried and failed in the past, but it's time to get back up. It's time to make a decision not to dwell on past failures. Try again! It may just work out this time!

I don't know what your mountain is. Your mountain could be finances, low self-esteem, addictions, doubt, unbelief, the list could go on.

Whatever the mountain is, know that God is big enough to fix it if you make a decision to pursue your passion again.

It's time for you to step on those mountains and crush them forever! You must make a decision to move beyond the limitations of your mind! It's time to make the decision to break free from the hindrances that have caused your gift to lie dormant. You must press past fears! Your victory over these mountains will happen when you make the decision to believe what God has said about you!

Untie yourself, you great big elephant you!

CHAPTER THREE

YOU HAVE POWER AND DOMINION

And God said, Let us make man in our image,
after our likeness: and let them have dominion
over the fish of the sea, and over the fowl of the
air, and over the cattle, and over all the earth,
and over every creeping thing that creepeth
upon the earth. Genesis 1:26

Power is having the ability to act or produce an effect. This means God has given you the legal authority to rule and reign in this earth realm. Dominion is the supreme authority or sovereignty, rule or control and absolute ownership.

God has given you power over all things on earth including the enemy or Satan. Satan attempts to steal your dominion. He wants to enslave you to the bondage of your past.

The thief cometh not, but for to steal, and to kill, and to destroy: I am come that they might have life, and that they might have it more abundantly. John10:10

According to this passage the enemy or thief's job is to steal, kill and destroy us at all cost. He will do anything to keep us bound to dead situations.

Because he is not omnipotent he has to employ others to help him do his dirty work. Ephesians 6:12 says "For we wrestle not against flesh and blood, but against principalities, against powers, against the rulers of the darkness of this world, against spiritual wickedness in high places."

This scripture tells of the additional forces the enemy uses to stop us from walking in purpose.

FEAR

One of the biggest tactics the enemy uses is fear. Fear immobilizes and causes you to become stuck in place. The enemy uses fear of failure and rejection to keep you from trying to accomplish your dreams and goals. Faith is necessary if you expect to believe God and defeat the enemy.

> Behold, I give unto you power to tread on serpents and scorpions, and over all the power of the enemy: and nothing shall by any means hurt you. Luke 10:19

God has given us power and dominion over the tactics of the enemy! Circumstances, situations, and obstacles will arise, but you don't have to let them determine your destiny!

You do not have to feel like you are stuck in a dead-end job, negative environment, or abusive relationships. You don't have to accept being broke. God wants you to dominate or rule over your relationships, etc.

Your hands are not tied as long as you have blood running through your veins. You have the power to change your present status. Consider these scriptures found in 2 Kings.

2Ki 7:3 And there were four leprous men at
the entering of the gate; and they said one to
another, Why sit we here until we die?
2Ki 7:4 If we say, We will enter into the city,
then the famine is in the city, and we shall die
there: and if we sit still here, we die also. Now
therefore come, and let us fall unto the host of
the Syrians: If they save us alive, we shall live;
and if they kill us, we shall but die.

The Bible goes on to tell how the leprous men went
into the city despite their fears and found that the Lord
caused an evacuation of the Syrians. God had not only
caused the people of the city to leave, but He did it in a way
that caused them to leave all of their possessions. These
possessions became bounty for the courageous lepers.

You must believe you have power and dominion over
the circumstances and situations in your life. If you are not
satisfied with the way your life is going change it! God has
already given you the authority to make a decision to change
the outcome of your current situation.

You must understand that you do not have to wait until
you get to Heaven to enjoy the goodness of God. You can
experience His goodness right here on earth!

YOU possess the power to change your destiny! Yes,
you can start your own business! Yes, you do have what it
takes to create a new invention! You have been empowered
by God to make your dreams come true! God has already
blessed you with the ability to change the outcome of every
situation or circumstance in your life! You were created for
success!

You have dominion! With God on your side you cannot
be defeated!

CHAPTER FOUR

ENEMIES OF SUCCESS

Not until we identify and understand the
attitudes and conditions that threaten our
success can we take the steps necessary to
overcome them.
~Sun Tzu

There are enemies of success that lie deep within us as
humans. Listed below are several characteristics, attitudes and
bad habits that become a part of our daily lives. Destroying
these unhealthy traits will help you become successful.

Lack of setting clear goals. Unclear goals can cause failure
and confusion. Goals must be measureable and attainable.
Setting unrealistic goals can be dangerous and damaging to
your self-esteem. Goals also must be written down so that
you can refer to them frequently.

Lack of a planning. There is an adage that says "If you fail
to plan then you plan to fail." Lack of planning is the enemy
of success. If you do not set a step-by-step plan on how to
achieve the goals you have set, you may become frustrated
when your goal does not appear to be reached. Planning is
necessary to keep your business from being disorganized.
Start making a plan now!

Lack of discipline. Discipline is vitally important for
anyone expecting to build wealth. The first discipline that
business owners and individuals must develop is learning to
manage your debt-to-income ratio. You must save more than
you spend. Many people miss opportunities because they do

not have the money to invest when the time comes.

Inconsistency. In order to produce results you must be consistent. You have to get up and press when you don't feel like it. And you can never let the success you had yesterday cause you to be slack today.

Lack of focus. Focus teaches you to fix your eyes on your goal or target. Focus also teaches you to recognize distractions.

Lack of enthusiasm. Lack of enthusiasm can cause you to get bored with your goals. You must be determined and take initiative in this pursuit to obtain your dreams.

Laziness. Laziness breeds poverty. Lazy people spend most of their time wanting and daydreaming instead of putting forth the effort to make their dreams come true. Laziness can cause someone to become a hater of other People's success.

Indifference. Indifference is having a lack of concern about your future. Writing a new vision for your life, family or business will help you overcome indifference.

Rigidity. Rigidity is having a closed mind about new opportunities. Getting stuck on the procedure of doing things a certain way can result in the loss of great advice that could have landed you great success. Stay open-minded.

Complacency. Complacency can cause you to be comfortable with your situation. Reaching for new goals can help you overcome complacency.

Procrastination. Procrastination is when we postpone what needs to be done today until tomorrow. Procrastination slows down success and causes a person to think they have time to fix an issue later. Procrastination is a bad habit that can eat your drive and determination. Make a list of tasks you've been putting off and accomplish at least one TODAY!

Indecision. Indecision or the inability to make a clear decision can cause you to miss out on great opportunities.

Now that you know some of the enemies of success, you must begin to sever them from your life. The counterattack to all of these enemies is action. It's time to actively pursue the enemies that have held you bound.

CHAPTER FIVE

REMOVING EXCUSES
No one ever excused his way to success.
~Dave Del Dotto

Can you imagine Jesus, our Great Lord and Savior, sitting in the roughest street of your community telling God all the reasons He couldn't die for our sins?

What would have happened if Jesus made all the excuses we make today? I shudder to think of our expected end if Jesus did not take the weight of our sins upon his shoulders.

If you plan to be successful in life, you must remove the excuses you made in the past. Every time you justify or make up a reason why you have not done something you are giving yourself permission to stay in a broken situation. Excuses only satisfy laziness and laziness produces nothing.

You must take responsibility for your present reality. Rehearsing all the different ways you failed in the past does not fix or change anything. You must move past the corridors of your mind and put your ideas and thoughts into action!

Remember, it is not someone else's responsibility to make your dreams come true! God gave you an assignment to carry out and if you don't make it happen, you will be at fault.

DO SOMETHING!

It's time to take control of your destiny! You possess gifts and talents that can change your life. Locked away in you are solutions to problems people are looking for every day. You may have a vision for an improvement for some product that's already out on the market that could land you billions of dollars! There may be someone waiting to donate millions of dollars to fund the charity you always wanted to start! You may be sitting on an idea for a business that could be a Fortune 500 company!

If you don't want your life to look the same next year, you have to do something different now. See yourself moving ahead and becoming the person you always wanted to be, and then act on it! Yes, you can do it!

YOU HAVE EVERYTHING YOU NEED! STOP PROCRASTINATING!

You have everything you need to fulfill your purpose. If you are not sure what your first step should be you can visit the library or search the internet for information about the subject.

How many times have you said to yourself, I am going to write a book after I finish school? Or I will write this book as soon as everything in my life calms down. Life never calms down, it just keeps on going. Time waits for no one.

Situations are going to just keep happening. You might as well write about it as you go! Who knows, your story may just be the next New York Bestseller!

Remember, procrastination is an enemy of success. Get started! Stop procrastinating!

NO LIMITS, NO BOUNDARIES

There are no limits and boundaries to how high you can soar! Anything is possible for those who believe! There is no box that can enclose you. You can make a decision to remove the excuses that have hindered you.

You do not have to settle for less! You do not have to live from paycheck to paycheck!

You are blessed and talented enough to buy yourself out of working for someone else! You are smart enough! God has planted greatness on the inside of you! He has said you are above and not beneath! You are the head and not the tail! You are an overcomer! Whose report will you believe?

I remember a time in my life when my husband and I seemed to be experiencing hardship at an astronomical level. Our previous landlord suddenly decided to sell the house we were renting from him. So that we could save money, we moved our family into an affordable one bedroom apartment with all bills paid.

The first few months we paid the rent with no problem. However, in the fourth month we experienced difficulties and could not pay the rent.

Without knowing our situation, one of our mentors said to my husband, "You are going to be so grateful for what God is about to do in your life in the next year. You will look back on what you are going through now and wonder how you ever allowed yourself to be in this situation."

Of course at that time we did not know what he meant by that statement. The following weeks after receiving the word from our mentor my husband and I realized that we couldn't make the money quick enough to stop eviction.

Later, we realized we allowed ourselves to be evicted. There were numerous things we could have done to pay our rent. We could have done something to keep our apartment.

We could have made dinners and sold them for $7.00 a plate. Most of the people in the apartment complex worked long hours and would have loved a home cooked meal. There were at least 300 apartments in the complex. If only half of our neighbors ordered a plate we would have made over $1,000.00.

We could have charged an affordable fee to clean homes. Cleaning four homes a week for $100 would have been $1,600 a month minus cleaning supplies.

We could have babysat kids. Instead we did nothing. Consequently we lost our apartment, but we learned a valuable lesson. We allowed the situation to happen the way it did. We made the wrong choice, which was to sit there and die.

Are you guilty of allowing your circumstances to be the way they are? You can change it!

HOW BAD DO YOU WANT IT?

The question is not and has never been "If" you can achieve your goals and dreams, you were created to win! The question is how bad do you want it? What are you willing to sacrifice to get what you want? Are you willing to give up your free time to achieve success? Are you willing to educate yourself concerning your purpose? Will you make time to perfect your gift every day?

Achieving your goals will take extra effort. It may mean you have to wake up an hour earlier in the morning or go to sleep an hour later in the evening. Making a commitment to pursue your goals may mean you can't always go to the movies or shopping with your friends.

Here is a shocking reality; many people do nothing with the dream or idea that has been given to them. As a result they see the idea God gave them flash across the television screen with someone else's name on it! Imagine how you would feel if that happened to you.

There is no feeling worse than seeing someone else capitalize on a dream or vision God gave to you!

IT'S YOUR TURN

If you have been preparing for success and it just seems like nothing is happening for you, hold on. If God said it, it will come to pass. God is not a man that He should lie (Numbers 23:19). He must fulfill every promise He made you. Remember, there is nothing too hard for God!

If you have not taken your first step into purpose, now is the time to move! Stop waiting on someone or something to materialize your dream for you! You have everything you need! Don't wait until tomorrow, next week or next year to accomplish your dreams! It's time for you to prosper! Your idea or business can be a reality! It's your turn! The time is now!

CHAPTER SIX

PLAN TO SUCCEED

He who fails to plan, plans to fail.
~Author unknown

Congratulations on making it to this chapter! Hopefully you have made a decision to bury every excuse that has caused you to be immobile.

Planning to succeed requires you to have a plan of action. The key to success is preparation. Success loves preparation. To succeed, you must be ready when opportunities come your way. You never know who you may run into from day to day, but it is better to be prepared than to miss your opportunity.

MAKE A PLAN

"The secret of success in life is for a man to
be ready for his opportunity when it comes."
~Benjamin Disraeli

In preparing to make your dreams become a reality, you must have a plan. The Bible tells us to write the vision and make it plain and God will make it come to pass.

And the Lord answered me, and said, write the vision, and make it plain upon tables, that he may run that readeth it. Habakkuk 2:2

Having a plan will:

1) Help you stay focused.
2) Help you be effective and productive.
3) Eliminate frustration.
4) Eliminate missed opportunities
5) Eliminate confusion.
6) Help you be more organized.

Many challenges and distractions will come to stop you from pursuing your destiny. Making a plan will help you stay focused. Referring to your plan during times of discouragement and frustrations will help you stay on track. Take the time to write your plan down so you can reflect on it when necessary.

SET GOALS

"If you don't know where you're going, you'll
wind up somewhere else." ~Yogi Berra

After you make a plan, you will need to set goals. Setting goals will help you achieve success. Goals give you clear and precise direction. Setting goals keep you motivated and also help you to measure your progress.

Remember to set goals that are clear and achievable. Setting unrealistic goals can cause you to fail before you begin.

GET READY TO WORK

I've always believed that if you put in the
work, the results will come.
~Michael Jordan
Accomplishing your goals is going to take hard work. Roll up your sleeves and get ready to get your hands dirty! If you have a dream, it is your responsibility to bring it to pass!

BE PERSISTENT

If you live long enough, you'll make mistakes. But if you
learn from them, you'll be a better person. It's how you
handle adversity, not how it affects you. The main thing is
never quit, never quit, never quit. ~ Bill Clinton

You are going to have to be persistent to achieve your
goals. You have to be as aggressive as a pit bull about your
dreams. Don't give up when someone tells you no; everyone
will not believe in your dream.

MAKE A COMMITMENT

All promise outruns performance. ~Ralph
Waldo Emerson

If you have commitment issues, now is the perfect time to
get rid of them. Once you make a commitment to achieve
your goals you have to be prepared to stick to it.
Accomplishing the goals you set will have to become one of
the top priorities in your life.

BE CONFIDENT

If you want to reach a goal, you must "see the reaching"
in your own mind before you actually arrive at your goal.
~Zig Zeglar

Believe in yourself! If you do not believe in you, why should
anyone else? Would you invest in you? You have to look the
part and play the part. First impressions are lasting
impressions. Chances are you will not get a second chance to
make a first impression

CHAPTER SEVEN

ACTIVATION
Faith is the currency used in the Kingdom of God.
~Author unknown

God has given us the power to obtain success and wealth! Wealth is not just about having money, it's about living and enjoying life to the fullest. You obtain wealth when you find and fulfill your purpose.

Abundance and prosperity are characteristics of God's blessings in our lives. God wants you to be His role model on the earth. He wants you to represent Him in everything you do. Your life should mirror the success and wealth that God intended for you! You do not have to live in poverty! Jesus has already made intercession on your behalf. He died just so that you could have a better quality of life.

You can change your circumstances by activating the power of God to move in your life! God is moved when you exercise faith. Moving in faith will provoke Him to move on your behalf.

WHAT IS FAITH AND HOW TO GET IT?

Now, Faith is the substance of things hoped for, the evidence of things not seen. Hebrews 11

Having faith means you believe and trust everything God has said about your situation. Seeking

God builds faith. Because God is The King, we as his children are royalty and reside in his domain. Because we are royalty there are certain rights and benefits afforded to us.

Before you can understand or identify what your benefits are, you need to study the Word of God and spend time in prayer. When you read and spend time talking with God, you build an intimate relationship with Him. As your relationship grows, your faith in Him grows and your understanding of what His will for your life is, increases.

> Seek ye first the kingdom of God and His
> Righteousness and all these things shall be
> added unto you. Mathew 6:33

Reading God's word will activate your faith! Application of God's Word demands positive changes in your life! Remember, faith cometh by hearing and hearing the Word of God (Romans 10:17). This means that the more you hear, read, and study God's word, the stronger your belief or faith will become. You will begin to have an understanding of the gifts God placed in you. Reading and studying
scriptures will also give you strength and courage to carry out God's will for your life.
You must remember we serve a big and mighty God who can do all that we are able to ask or think!

HELPFUL SCRIPTURES ON FAITH

Now Faith is the substance of things hoped
for, the evidence of things not seen.
Hebrews 11:1

I can do all things through Christ who
strengthens me. Philippians 4:13

We do not walk by sight but by faith.
2 Corinthians 5:7

Verily, I say unto you, He that
believeth on me, the works that I do shall he do
also; and greater works than these shall he do;
because I go unto my Father. And whatsoever
ye shall ask in my name, that will I do, that the
Father may be glorified in the Son. If ye shall ask
anything in my name, I will do it. John 14:12 -14

All things are possible to those who believe.
Mark 9:23

Faith cometh by hearing and hearing the
WORD of God. Romans 10:17

SOW YOUR WAY INTO YOUR BLESSING

Give, and it shall be given unto you; good measure, pressed down, and shaken together, and running over, shall men give into your bosom. For with the same measure that ye mete withal it shall be measured to you again. Luke 6:38

You can activate God's promises in your life by sowing seeds A seed is not your tithe. Your tithe to God is 10% of whatever income you receive. Your tithe is a requirement; it's what you owe God (Malachi 3:8-10). A seed is whatever you give beyond your tithe. You can sow seeds of time, gifts, talent, or money. Seed activates your faith and makes a demand on the promises of God.

You can sow your way into a blessing. When you sow money into a ministry it is for your benefit. When you give above your tithes, you are putting a demand on God to perform miracles in your life.

PRAISE IS OUR MOST POWERFUL WEAPON

You can praise your way through every situation! Giving God praise is when we verbally or physically thank Him for all that He has done for us. Giving God praise when your situations look dreary is another way to show Him you believe that He is able to do anything.

Praise can be done in several different ways. Some people dance, sing, or jump to give God praise. Others play music, cry or lift their hands to show God how much they adore Him.

Praising God is a powerful weapon. It is said that praise confuses the enemy. The enemy doesn't understand how you can still praise God when everything in your life seems to be going wrong.

If you want to activate blessings in your life, praise God continuously. As a result God will move mountains on your behalf.

PRAYING AND FASTING

Praying is vitally important. Prayer is simply talking to God. God is most moved when we open up our mouths and tell him all of our concerns. He tells us in 1 Peter 5:7 to cast all of our cares upon Him because He cares for us.
God wants us to give him our problems. He is the supplier of everything we could ever need in life.

Seek God so that you can know His will for your life. Consult with God and He will give you step-by-step instructions on how to go about obtaining success.

God told Joshua to sanctify himself so that he could go in and possess the land (Joshua 1:1-8). In other words, God was telling Joshua to fast and pray, so he would not deliberate on what God said to do.

God tells us to fast and pray so that our minds will be ready to receive or act when necessary. Fasting and praying helps us to see an opportunity in what others may see as a waste of time.

All great businesses start with an idea. God sends ideas to us daily. The test is; believing you are capable through Jesus to make the thought reality. You are the representative God has chosen to carry out His agenda. God wants to use you to make the thought or idea physically exist on earth

CHAPTER EIGHT

OPEN UP YOUR MOUTH!

Words have power, presence and prophetic
implications with no geographical limitations.
~Dr. Cindy Trimm

The words we speak determine our success and failure.
God said in Genesis 1:3, "Let there be light" and the light
appeared! God has made us in His image and given us the
power to speak life in every area of our lives.

The Bible says that we have to speak things the way we
want them to be not as they are. Thou shalt also decree a
thing, and it shall be established unto thee: and the light shall
shine **upon thy ways. Job 22:28**

God has given us the power to decree and declare. To
decree means to issue a rule of law and to declare means to
proclaim. We can issue a degree and legislate laws that govern
the earth realm with the authority given to us by God. As we
make decrees, the atmosphere and earth have to obey our
command.

God instructs us to pull down everything that exalts
itself above His wisdom and knowledge.

Casting down imaginations, and every high
the thing that exalts itself against the knowledge
of God, and bringing into captivity every
thought to the obedience of Christ.
2Corinthians 10:5

In the book "Commanding Your Morning" Dr. Cindy Trimm
teaches on the importance and power of decreeing and

declaring. Her book provides powerful declarations that will unleash the power of God in your life!

> Death and life are in the power of the
> tongue and they that love it shall eat the fruit
> thereof. Proverbs 18:21

You must learn how to bless yourself and others. Start saying good things about yourself and those around you. Start saying the things God has said about you.

DON'T FORGET ABOUT GOD

Once God blesses you as He has promised, it's imperative that you never forget that He gave you the power to get wealth (Deuteronomy 8). Never forget where you came from.

Apply the Golden Rule to all areas of your life; "treat people how you want to be treated." Remember, God trusts you with His Kingdom. Don't do anything to misrepresent him. You have a job to do! God wants you to tell everybody how He blessed you. God wants and deserves all the glory.

> And they overcame him by the blood of the
> Lamb, and the words of their testimony, and
> they love not their lives unto death. Revelation
> 12:11

Don't procrastinate! Go get the blessings God promised you! You don't have to wait until tomorrow!

Tomorrow may not come! Get moving on fulfilling your destiny! THE TIME IS NOW!

ABOUT THE AUTHOR

"E. Moore (Ebony Moore) is an award-winning author/illustrator with over 60 titles in print. Moore developed a love for writing and illustrating when she was five years old and has been writing ever since.

Mrs. Moore has created books in a variety of genres. While most of her books are children's books, she has also written novels and spiritual self-help books.

Moore continues to create educational resources that pour into the lives of others. She travels the world speaking at schools, conferences, and other educational events inspiring others to unlock the potential they possess.

For more information about this author please visit www.ebonymoore.com.